Philosophical Chronicles

John D. Caputo, *series editor*

PERSPECTIVES IN
CONTINENTAL
PHILOSOPHY

JEAN-LUC NANCY

Philosophical Chronicles

Translated by Franson Manjali

FORDHAM UNIVERSITY PRESS
New York ■ 2008

Philosophical Chronicles was originally published in French as *Chroniques philosophiques*, by Jean-Luc Nancy, Copyright © Éditions Galilée, 2004.

Library of Congress Cataloging-in-Publication Data

Nancy, Jean-Luc.
[Chroniques philosophiques. English]
Philosophical chronicles / Jean-Luc Nancy ; translated by Franson Manjali.
    p.   cm.—(Perspectives in continental philosophy series)
Includes bibliographical references.
ISBN-13: 978-0-8232-2758-7 (pbk. : alk. paper)
1. Philosophy, Modern—21st century.   I. Title.
B792.N3513   2008
194—dc22

                                        2007046913

This work has been published with the assistance of the French Ministry of Culture—National Center for the Book.

Ouvrage publié avec le concours du Ministère français chargé de la culture—Centre National du Livre.

Contents

Philosophical Chronicles

These eleven chronicles were broadcast on the radio between September 2002 and July 2003, on the last Friday of each month, as part of France Culture's program "Philosophy Fridays." The broadcast was directed, on behalf of the Collège International de Philosophie, by François Noudelmann, whom I thank for his invitation.

The texts published here correspond almost exactly to the texts that were actually delivered (and recorded for the Web site and the archives of France Culture). In each case, the context of speech led to some improvisation; some of these changes were written down and are reproduced here, others remain only in the spoken version.

The musical accompaniment for the chronicles, suggested by François Noudelmann, was the aria "In lagrime stemprato il cor qui cade," from Antonio Caldara's *Maddalena ai piedi di Cristo*.

Some of these chronicles have been published in several issues of *Rue Descartes*, the journal of the Collège International de Philosophie.

Translator's Foreword

This book, comprising texts of monthly talks or "chronicles" presented over a period of eleven months on France Culture radio, connects up philosophy with several nodes of contemporary life. The chronicles of an old discipline—perhaps the oldest living discipline—cannot but relate the chronic problems and crises it faces in its very act of survival. Though philosophy's very existence depends on its being unconditioned, in its course of development, philosophers tend to submit it to various conditionalities, including a cultural conditionality that is much in vogue today. However, philosophy lives and survives its crises by continually withdrawing itself from all given conditionalities, without ever being able to hook itself onto any permanent notion of the unconditioned. The rhythm or the pulsation of philosophy always takes it outside of itself, opens it toward what Nancy calls the "time of thought," where it encounters the "absolutely non-given." These chronicles point to a chronic opening up of philosophy toward the undecidable time to come.

The movement toward an unknown exterior that philosophy requires today is not merely of a temporal kind. Behind the current crisis (certainly not a "clash," as it is claimed) of civilizations manifest in unprecedented religious and nationalist fervors or global capitalist maneuverings, Nancy identifies the aging of a culture of autonomy. As the autonomous form of life and the associated auto-motive techniques of this culture are approaching senility, philosophy may well suggest the reinvention of an entire mode of existence. *Exonomy* is the name that Nancy gives to this alternative law or mode of existence, distinct from heteronomy but conceptually akin to exogamy. The space of exonomy is outside the space of both self and other; it is an in-between space, always not yet given.

If philosophy can guide us into another time and another space, what, then, is it to life? Is philosophy a part of it, or outside? Does it guide the conduct of life or stand aloof as a conceptual guide? Is it of the order of actions or of reasons? All such questions and the tensions to which they give rise are internal to philosophy, according to Nancy, making philosophy something like an intimate "form of life." It is not, however, a prior form, available either transcendentally or empirically, but it appears out of life itself as its possible formation. Philosophy inserts itself into and emerges from the space of discourses already given, whether of religion, of the quotidian, or of politics, science, or art; it is the spacing of these discourses. As spacing, its sense exceeds every given sense, not only in and of life, but even in death, and of death.

The question of philosophy's response to religion—one of the most ancient and most profound aspects of civilizational existence—is posed in the context of the renewed war cries in the name of religion in the contemporary world. Nancy analyzes the problem in terms of the very character of monotheism: in the name of a single and all-encompassing god, it abandons man to solitude in a state of godlessness. And then it seeks to "gather" these abandoned human beings into the totality and universality of a newly found truth. Even while colonial expansions and conquests are undertaken in the name of truth, the bogus assurance of religious salvation is still held forth, only reinforcing man's abandonment. Such is the context that demands a deconstruction of monotheism, in order to extract what is repressed in it, denied by it, and left outside its own totality.

The decline of the meaning of the word *politics* is not of a different kind. In the politically charged world of today, where every sphere of life has necessarily become "political," nothing is seriously discerned as political, except in an overused sense of the word. The current critical sense of the word *political*, Nancy notes, was introduced recently in our languages, in order to understand the process behind what used to be considered the art of politics. In order to retrieve the specificity of a contemporary art of politics, we might well have to retreat from the current totalitarian notion of politics, as applying everywhere at all times.

The best example of a major philosopher going astray in his understanding of the conjunction between politics and history is Heidegger. Between politics' call for justice, and history's call for action, where have philosophers, at least since Hegel, put their stakes? And with what consequences? Can the mechanism of history and the affirmation of its struggle, perceived from the given position of the philosopher, usher in justice without subjecting the other to the will of the self? On this question foundered, not only Heidegger the reactionary, but perhaps various Marxisms too, though in different ways. How can the necessity of a politics of justice cope with the unfolding of historical events?

History's everyday events are even more difficult to interpret in a philosophical or political sense. Philosophers' dilemma, that is, when they have to deal with the everyday, is in deciding whether mundane daily events are to be inscribed into a higher level of—philosophical, historical, political, or aesthetic—sense, or left as insignificant. Though on occasion one can make some everyday events "appear," nonappearance is the essential mode of the everyday. It vascillates between hiding in the open and chance appearances in creative works. Yet now and then the everyday makes an unintended appearance in catastrophic and mortal events, such as earthquakes and wars. It is in such situations that an unmarked life is in silent contact with the nonapparent lives of all those who are living and dead, without this event ever rising beyond the level of everyday appearance.

The context of the ongoing war in Iraq is, for Nancy, the painful motivation for an inquiry into the meanings of words that govern contemporary national and global situations. Actions and denunciations on the basis of the prevailing sense of terms like *war, totalitarianism, democracy*, and so on will not do. This is because war now, more than ever before, is part and parcel of capitalist calculations and is aided by the augmentation of its technics. War is now part of capitalist production and management, a process without ends, save to increase its means. Even "democracy" is engineered for the sake of capital, whose politics is backed by a theology of foundational unity. Resistance to the avaricious war of a single theodemocracy will require more than an appeal to peace: we shall have to reinvent our cherished political words and alter their exhausted senses.

Perhaps this very notion of a "we" can be obtained only as negativity, as the affirmation of an impossible "we." In today's world, countless individuals die unseen, unattended, and unmourned. The increasing number of these "hidden deaths" is disconcerting, since human culture everywhere began by inscribing death in a social milieu. At the same time, modern society wants to offset the inexorable negativity by a sort of commercially viable positive attitude. Everywhere, even in the Hegelian dialectic, negativity must be transformed into a positivity. Rather than denying negativity—which is an undeniable part of life—either by rejecting it or by transforming it, the role of an "unemployed negativity" would be to affirm the other of what is merely possible, that is, to affirm the impossible. In this way, we can inscribe the hidden as well as distant deaths of others as "our" deaths.

The idea of "art," too, must continually integrate and acknowledge its every emerging form in every unfolding of time. Art as we understand it today is itself a relatively new invention—barely two centuries old—and it has been an invention of relentlessly proliferating senses. This external proliferation should be attributed to the ceaseless productivity of a desire situated in the very being of man: the desire for an overflow of meanings and a desire for what is yet to be sensed. This ceaseless denouement of senses yields, in parallel, varieties of "us" beyond our given sensible selves.

The concluding talk of the series, pronounced at the onset of France's devastatingly hot summer of

2003, is a discourse on the sun. The sun has been the source of numerous defining metaphors of the Occident—etymologically the place of the sun's decline or setting. The *Lumières* or the Enlightenment was, for the West, a reorienting toward the sun, given that *orient* means birth or sunrise. The play of light and darkness has been seminal in the progress of Western thought. Luminosity rules virtues like knowledge and beauty. The sun rules with its sharp edge of luminous bedazzlement. However, the Occident has also sought to avert the blinding power of the sun and to turn to the blind point behind it. This blind spot, Nancy notes, is indeed the source of its poetry.

I would like to acknowledge help and guidance received from the following sources: Aïcha Liviana Messina, who during her sojourn in New Delhi, took time off her research to correct an early draft of the translation; Myriam Rasiwala, a near-perfect French-English bilingual and translation specialist, who worked through every one of the constructional ambiguities in the original text; Jean-Luc Nancy, who while providing generous hospitality in his Strasbourg home, found time to discuss the sense of difficult philosophical expressions; the administration of the Maison des Sciences de l'Homme, Paris, where the major part of the translation was completed during the spring of 2006; and last but certainly not least, Jeff Fort, who did a remarkable job of vetting my final version of the translation.

I express my sincere gratitude to these individuals and the institution.

—Franson Manjali

A chronicle of philosophy: What can this really mean? A chronicle is a rubric indicating something punctual and periodical, whose content has to do either with a particular specialization (gastronomy, gardening, etc.), or with a subjectivity (the world according to the mood of the chronicler). But philosophy, in whatever manner we envisage it, aspires to be removed from specialization as well as from subjectivity. From the beginning and in principle, it demands the universal and the objective. That is to say, it asks how the universal can be an object of thought and how any object, whatever it may be, can be thought according to the universal. Thus, even if thought adopts the principle of multiplicity, heterogeneity, and the incommensurability of beings, it still thus posits a form of universal object.

Kant had a word for this: "the unconditional." Reason demands the unconditional. That is its passion. It demands that which does not depend on anything prior, on any condition already posited. If I admit a condition, a prior given, I cannot begin to philosophize.

How, then, can this exigency be made to vary in the course of a chronicle? Either universal objectivity is given, and it cannot vary. Or else it is only a vague and inconsistent disposition, a porridge of "values," "virtues," and common sense that can be warmed up and dished out on every occasion. Today there is a cultural mode of "philosophy" that endlessly warms up this very light broth, while letting the vague promise of an unconditional final truth float about in its vapor. Thus one entertains a cheap ethico-pragmatic consensualist ideology while boosting the market value quoted for "the philosopher."

I do not claim that I can avoid the cultural peril without remainder or without risk. I have chosen to brush up against such ambiguity because this cultural danger must be confronted on its own territory—by speaking on the radio, for example. This is not just a matter of strategy. It is also because the cultural development of philosophy itself opens up a question of some philosophical importance.

Indeed, the cultural development of philosophy has this importance because it is in fact a chronic illness of philosophy (and I will also take up the word *chronic* from this angle).[1] There have always been Platonisms, Stoicisms, Averroisms, or Kantianisms, idealisms or utilitarianisms, which configured the opinions and the *media* of their times, salons, schools, and political offices. These conformist assurances become eroded and collapse on a regular basis. But why these chronic crises—these crises in the chronicles of philosophy?

The reason for them is itself chronic. The exigency of the unconditioned regularly allows what is simply unacceptable in it to fall back and to become fixed in a preconditioned consensus. This chronic pulsation, or even illness, is the alternation between an unacceptable demand and the responses destined to disappoint it or to betray it.

Why is the demand unacceptable? Not because of any philosophical heroism (Socrates against the power of the Sophists, Descartes against Scholastic might), but by virtue of an internal constitution. Philosophy demands the unconditional because it is itself the effect of a withdrawal from given conditions.

Philosophers, Marx said, do not emerge from the earth like mushrooms. Philosophy is not the result of a "Greek miracle" or of a sudden revelation of the *logos*. It is born out of a withdrawal from the conditions found in a world of gods, sacrifices, hierarchies, hieroglyphs, and hierophanies. It is born out of a withdrawal of the reasons of the world. Philosophy represented what remained without reason as Being stripped bare, or as the *logos*, and later as the certainty of the subject, or as transcendental intentionality, or as history, and so on. But in each case, what the desire for reason in reality translates is this: that the world has entered into the absence of reason.

What has since then become chronic—or subject to a chronicle—is the compulsion to demand an unconditional where, in effect, every given, every origin, every filiation is withdrawn. The unconditioned is demanded because we are in fact without a given condition. There remains only, if we can put it thus, the gift in a pure state: the world, history, and man as gifts that nothing precedes.

What was called "the death of God" and later "the end of metaphysics," or even "the end of philosophy," consisted in bringing to light the following: there is no first or last condition; there isn't any unconditioned that can be the principle or the origin. But this "there isn't" is unconditioned, and there you have, if I dare say, our "human condition."

That is how the possibility of chronic crises, in which one philosophy succeeds another, comes to an end, in a sense. That is how a turning point is initiated. But if philosophy can no longer be the chronic disease of a succession of ideologies, then it must understand its own constitution differently.

For it is no longer a matter of curing an illness. Some people believe that it is, and they think that it is enough to hold onto what is reasonable and to the discourses that are capable of validating their own meanings. However, reason wants more than the reasonable, and truth is beyond every validated or sensible meaning. Here there is a certainty that is also chronic: it opens up before us, once again, the time of thought. The nongiven, the absolutely non-given, that is to say, the gift of being in which existence without reason demands its due—which is incalculable and is not even due . . .

27 September 2002

For this second chronicle, I will be a chronicler in the sense that I will try, albeit as a philosopher, to address aspects of our current situation that, if they are not altogether immediate, are at least those of the present day in the broad sense. I mean the current situation of murderous and/or financial terror against the background of an overvaluation of God (whatever name he is given) and a devaluation of money (that of the shareholders, but even more the money of those who do not have any). This situation needs to be considered in a philosophical chronicle because it constitutes a *philosophical* actuality.

Hegel wrote—this is his famous sentence about the owl of Minerva—that philosophy appears when a form of life has become old. Since late antiquity, there has never been a growing-old as manifest as ours. The capitalist economy accumulates impasses, abscesses, and uncontrollable disorders. The society it governs does not believe in itself anymore. Words and concepts that were still valid fifteen years ago, like "the rule of law," "human rights," and "democracy," are losing visibly and on a daily basis their practical as well as theoretical and symbolic credibility. Scientific, technical, juridical, and moral progress immediately displays, at every step, ambivalences that suspend the name "progress," and along with it, those of "humanity," "reason," and "justice."

That's when one brandishes idols, that is to say, ideas reduced to a kind of belch. On one side, "God's will," on the other, "human freedom." These expressions provide a front, of course, for large-scale maneuvers aimed at seizing power and wealth. But this front is marked with figures of identification (or rather, of subjection) and of mobilization (or rather, of compulsive repetition). And these figures are painted on bombs.

God, man, will, freedom: who does not see that these are the four terms of a metaphysical order whose combinations saturate the horizon of a world of autonomy? The form of life that has grown old is that of autonomy. Autonomy of premise, autocracy of choice and of decision, auto-management of the identical, auto-production of value, of sign and of image, auto-reference of discourse, all these are used up, exhausted, just as the automobile, when one takes a closer look, is already given over to senility.[2]

To speak of a "clash of civilizations" is a sign of thoughtlessness. It is the same civilization that exploits oil and the God of Abraham and Jefferson, that declares us all equal and leaves each one to fend for himself, that pretends to cheat death by phantasm or by denial. Civilization of self-sufficiency, of self-satisfaction—and of self-division.

Discerning what is happening, the aging of a culture of autonomy that at the same time forms the ethical and symbolic baggage of globalization (yes, it is an old animal that is globalizing), does not provide any means of action, but should allow us to imagine where to look, if this is possible, for the signs of another youth.

It seems to me that we might at least say this: we will not oppose autonomy with heteronomy, with which it forms a pair. Being heteronomous toward another subject that is itself autonomous changes nothing, regardless of whether this other autonomous thing is named god, the market, technics, or life. But, in order to open a new path, we could try out the word *exonomy*. This word would evoke a law that would not be the law of the same or of the other, but one that would be unappropriable by either the same or the other. Just as *exogamy* goes outside of kinship, *exonomy* moves out of the binary familiarity of the self and the other.

This would be a law always linked to the outside of law, of which we have a few images from the past in the *Moira* of the Greeks,[3] in the election of Abraham, in Dante's Beatrice, or in Hamlet's lucid madness. These are sharply contrasting, even contradictory images. But they all sketch an outside that is not an autonomy, that is not a mastery, that is neither the same nor the other. These are not clear images, I know, and besides, they too have grown old. That is why we must, for today, dryly and enthusiastically give the last word to Beckett: "Imagination dead, imagine."

25 October 2002

Is philosophy a form of life? Or, according to an expression closer to Aristotle than to Wittgenstein, does philosophy give form to life? This question immediately receives two opposite responses. Yes, according to one *doxa* or a widespread feeling that philosophy should give meaning and strengthen a conduct regulated by this meaning. No, responds the opposite sentiment, which sees philosophy as the practice of a discourse of meaning or truth, but by right or in fact deprived of any mobilizing energy.

Both of these postulations are to be found among philosophers. Descartes holds that one should philosophize very little, but with the goal of firmly ascertaining the reasons for acting in the world, in life, by way of medicine, mechanics, and morality. Heidegger, by contrast, declares, even as he speaks of putting existence into play, that one should not believe that this putting into play will be effective in the book that speaks about it.

In one case, one supposes that the order of reasons generates energy, and in the other, one affirms that the effectivity of this energy is of an order different from the order of reasons. One thus poses the problem of the passage from one order to the other.

There are periods and figures of philosophy in which the indication of a form of life is quite vivid: in Stoicism and Epicureanism, for Schopenhauer and Nietzsche, and for others in whose work this indication loses visibility, as though veiled by concepts, analysis, and theory. "The concept or life"— this seems to be the alternative, about which it has been very common, in fact, to hear complaints made to the philosophers, who themselves sometimes add to the complaint and the anxiety about it.

We must note, rather, that this tension is *internal* to philosophy. No philosopher can ignore or disdain the form of life. But no philosopher—no one deserving the name *philosopher*—can assume that such a form is an idea, a schema that can be taken out of the drawer or the book and be applied on the street.

But this is not a matter of difficulties of application or mobilization. It concerns the fact that a philosopher immediately disqualifies the notions of both "form" and "life" understood as frame and content or even as signification and experience.

Neither of these notions is given at the beginning, nor for that matter, at the end. Philosophy consists precisely in working within a space where there is neither a configuration of meaning, nor a felt immediacy—nor, consequently, the possibility of mediating one through the other. In other words, neither the authority of religion nor that of "lived experience."

Between religion and lived experience—in a space, let us note, where one also finds politics, science, and art—philosophy has the task, if I may say so, of spacing as such. Neither form, nor life, nor concept, nor intuition, but from one to the other, or rather, from one within the other, through the other, but also one against the other, a tension without resolution. It is not a question of relieving this tension, for it delights in itself as much as it suffers from itself. Neither a modeling of life nor a pathos of the immediate. It is not a happy medium, it is the exacting sharp edge of the philosophical decision, that is, of an entire civilization.

But in confronting this, the philosopher understands that it is precisely life that is put into play and that may thus lose its way without any of the assurances provided by what is revealed or felt (or by some mixture of the two). It is a living being that philosophizes, and if life consists in being affected by itself, then in the act of philosophizing, it is affected by its own vacancy of sense. It takes, therefore, a certain form, and with it a certain force: the form and the force of holding oneself before this necessity—namely, that its meaning is never given to it, and that this is precisely what dictates its truth to it. A truth, consequently, that is never simply available but is always caught up in its own practice.

Transcribing the final proposition of Spinoza's *Ethics*, however roughly, we can therefore say that "sense is not the reward of philosophy, but its very practice." Thus philosophy is less a "form of life" than life forming itself, that is to say, thinking itself, in accordance with its excess over every given form or signification. Which also means, of course, this life thinking itself even in its death.

I recall that, one day when I was being transported in an ambulance, the driver asked me what my profession was. He then had this to say: "Philosophy—that should be of help to you in your present situation." At once I thought, almost in spite of myself, that basically he wasn't wrong. And I still think that in fact he was right, even if I don't know how to unravel this reasoning. But I also think at the same time that in this statement, my ambulance driver proved that he also is a philosopher. His confidence in philosophy, which one might well consider naive, contained an act of thought by which his life took form, transformed its ordinary form, just as it transformed my life at that same moment. The proof of this transformation is that I have not forgotten it.

22 November 2002

Today's theme will be monotheism. Why? I imagine that the motives are clear: the names of God, utterable or not, are invoked everywhere—*Allah akhbar!* In God we trust! *Yahweh Sabaoth! Dieu et mon droit!*—like emblazoned shields in the furious assault for domination. This domination does not even hide its stakes behind religious pretexts, since it now seems clear that the security and the dignity of existence would have an interest in reference to religion, and that one god would be inseparable from the freedom of comfort just as another is from the cry of poverty, while a third would provide the guarantee of a state after having promised a territory.

The wars of old were the deeds of princes. Each one brandished his religious banner, but it happened at some distance from the people. I would even exaggerate and say: the parishes or the common people were not directly affected. Today, the technical and economic forces struggling for global mastery or servitude are reinforced by religious or spiritual forces in the sense that these words henceforth signify issues that no longer bear upon "nations," "classes," or "peoples": life lived in spite of its harshness, the recognition of the self in spite of its uncertainty, in short, a condition not of "sense" but of a sustained decision to exist.

It was in fact this new phenomenon (or what seemed like a new phenomenon) that led Michel Foucault, twenty-three years ago, to salute the "will to renew the whole of one's existence," which he claimed had swept through the Iranian people when they rose up against their former regime. We must not be too quick to laugh at him; rather, we should closely reread his statements of this period. This does not mean, however, that he was able to think through what was being played out there in its implication for monotheism. On the contrary, the rather conventional Marxism that he relied on undoubtedly limited his perspectives.

Whatever we make of this episode, today we can no longer avoid examining this supposedly religious reference. Indeed, the more important it becomes, the less we know what we are saying when we speak of religion, monotheism, or God, whether it is said in fits of exaltation or of denunciation.

Two questions arise: (1) How can we analyze monotheism *today*? (2) How do we understand and judge the mobilizations of which it is the object—or the subject?

I will merely lay out a few indications.

First of all, and fundamentally: Monotheism in the strictly Western sense is not the religion of a single god. "Western" here means what the Qur'an designates inclusively as "the people of the Book," Jews and Christians, together with Muslims, the spiritual stock of Abraham (still according to the Qur'an). It is not the religion of a single god as if it were a pantheon of gods reduced to a single entity. On the contrary, uniqueness eliminates every pantheon, as it does pantheism, and finally, strictly speaking, any theism. There is no more place for a particular being bearing the name "god," present, in its own proper mode, somewhere in this world or in another. With uniqueness, god loses his distinction as Being [*être*] or as a being [*étant*]. This god is not another god—he is neither other nor, therefore, the same in relation to other gods. He is, inasmuch as he *is*, the one who is not present. Nor is he absent (far away, elsewhere). He responds or corresponds, if I can put it this way, to the departure of all gods. The departure of the gods—the end of a world of agrarian and sacrificial cults, by all and for all—opened up a world (that of the cities, of commerce, of the alphabet) where the multiplicity of singulars involves the question of what Ibn 'Arabi calls "the one within the one." Man is henceforth alone, that is to say, strictly speaking, *atheist*, or godless. The ensemble of principles, both theistic and atheistic, is dismissed, for the sake of an anarchic position (in Schürmann's sense) of the singular existent. We might call this *absentheism*.

It is man abandoned to himself, without any means of rescue, without even any recourse to mourning a tragic destiny. Alone and lonely together, human beings are left to a condition stranger than fate or assurance: to a staggering enigma. If there is something divine in this, it is as the sign of this enigma. A god infinitely withdrawn, or even dispersed, the name of God written under erasure.

The second question has to do with the various mobilizations of monotheism. The response is necessarily double.

On the one hand, monotheism, born out of the desertion of the gods, hastens to remake the religious at the gates of the desert. Yet it is different, for it posits itself as *truth* and not, like the others, as assistance or as threat. Truth entails universality and totality: hence the expansionist and colonizing attitudes at the very moment when a distinction is drawn between the political and the religious. This is a new principle for war.

But on the other hand, the same postulation contradicts the anarchism of the totality of singular beings, and finally denies absen-theism for the sake of a hoax that holds up as "salvation" the exposure to abandonment that ought to be assumed as our own. Monotheism is the religion par excellence whose exclusion is internal to itself.

My conclusion will be brief: what remains for us is not to destroy monotheism (it does so on its own, by tearing itself apart), but to deconstruct it. That is to say, to extract from it, in spite of itself, what it conceals through ignorance, repression, or denial. We must retrace and furrow out the erasure of the divine name. We must push forward with the irreversible alteration of this name.

27 December 2002

Let's speak of "politics." I mean: let's speak of the word *politics* [*politique*].[4] It is no doubt a good and even a necessary means of speaking of the thing itself. Indeed, certain linguistic phenomena involving this word deserve our attention. To give an idea of what I intend to do, it is enough for me to point out the following: when I say, "let us speak of the word '*politique*,'" you do not know whether I am using the adjective or the substantive, or whether the latter is to be understood as feminine or masculine. Now, these trivial considerations involve several problems at once.

Let us begin with the adjective. An excessive use is made of it today when, in domains that are not in principle defined as "political," we affirm an essential political implication. In the artistic domain in particular, it is often seen as necessary to declare that a work or an intervention has a political relevance, a political sense, or even a political nature. Whereas in the past we would come across the notion of the political commitment of an artist (of a writer, a philosopher, or a scientist), today we must refer to a necessarily political dimension in their practice itself. What cannot be said to be "political" appears suspect in being *only* aesthetic, intellectual, technical, or moral. But what one calls "political," or the "political dimension," remains most of the time without any other precise definition. This is because the meaning of the word seems to be implicitly established: "political" would mean that which goes beyond all the particular delimitation of discipline and activity, operating at the level of the entire society (even that of humanity), of its conditions of existence and meaning. "Political" is thus invested with a potentially unlimited content.

This usage of the word derives from a more or less conscious belief in the idea that everything is or should be political. Now, this idea constitutes nothing other than the content of what one calls "totalitarianism." Many would be very vexed to learn that they speak—even if they do not think—in a "totalitarian" manner. However, it deserves to be said. Every time "political" refers to such a totalizing property, there is indeed "totalitarianism." That is to say, the horizon of this thought is that of a "political" absorption or assumption of every sphere of existence (I am pointing here more or less to a formula of the young Marx).

The simplest logic allows us to conclude that such an assumption of every sphere of existence in its entirety takes away the very specificity of the sphere of the assumption itself. If everything is political, then nothing is anymore. And this is perhaps in effect the real situation in which we find ourselves. But then we should no longer be able to speak of what is "political," except as an abuse of language and with a view to exploiting the accents—flattering, heroic, and charged with historical destiny—that are associated with this big word *political.*

That is, moreover, why the philosophical scene today is so intensely occupied with works that undertake to redefine and reanalyze the field and the sense of what is "political" in order thus to pull the word out of its dilution in what would have to be called social immanence.

What haunts the unreflective totalitarianism involved in the abuse of the term is in fact an obsession with the suppression of the separation. Everything must be political because politics as a separate sphere must be suppressed. Whether it is in the form of the state or that of parties, in the form of "politicking" or "the politician's politics" (a very remarkable tautology that one could analyze at length) or even that of subversive actions, every separate instance is now set to disappear—that is to say, quite naturally, every separate instance of communal existence. Communal existence must then, in the end, or at least in the regulative principle, ensure—on its own and as such—its own end, its sense and its fulfillment.

Now, this is precisely what must be placed in doubt, and it is indeed what we do in fact doubt, more or less consciously. The very people who claim that everything is political are often also those who think that democracy is not an end in itself and that our question is rather one of knowing toward what ends (or even toward what surpassing of the very idea of "end," which would involve another register of analysis) to direct it.

At this point we can touch upon another linguistic phenomenon. For a little over twenty years now, we have commonly spoken of "the political" [*le politique*], and this usage relegates "politics" [*la politique*] to the subordinate level of the execution of tasks (or even maneuvers). "The political" seems to represent the nobility of the thing—which thereby implicitly regains its specificity, and thus its relative separation.

We thus fail to recognize that this word in the masculine, a newcomer to the [French] language with this meaning, was introduced to refer to the concept or the essence of the political thing or domain—but precisely to the extent that this concept, or indeed this essence, required examination, analysis, interrogation. We began to speak of "the political" in this particular way from the moment we found it necessary to question the foundations of what we had previously called either the "science of government" or "public law." "The political" became the name of a problem, and one of no small importance. A problem of grounding, of foundation, or, on the contrary, the laying bare of an absence of depth. But it is also because of this problem that "politics" [*la politique*], losing all dignity as *art* in the old sense (of *technē*, of savoir faire), has become "politicking," whereas this art (of politics) was so noble and so powerful.

This is not the case in the personal vocabularies of the philosophers that I invoked a moment ago, each of whom questions, according to his own approach, either the masculine or the feminine, the essence or the art of the thing called politics / the political. My objective today was not to summon them—or the thing itself—to be judged. It was simply to suggest, very modestly, that we should not be using the terms *politics / the political* without at least trying to clarify what we are talking about. For, to be frank, the meaning of the word is lacking in our ordinary language, except in the form of a nebulous and totalitarian notion, in a consensually somnambulistic manner. But precisely this, the ordinary manner of speaking, produces political effects.

Political rigor and exactitude, today, begin with this critique of our language, even if we initially find it frustrating. How can we speak knowingly of "politics" and the "political"? I leave off deliberately with this question for today.

24 January 2003

Among the "affairs" that have cluttered our public scene for several years, there is one that is philosophical in nature. This is the famous "Heidegger affair" which it seems impossible seriously to clear away from the horizon or at least the backstage of the French intellectual scene. (For it must be noted that this is not always the case in other countries, far from it, a fact that also deserves to be analyzed.) Beyond the impressive collection of works that have been devoted to it, and that have also broadly exhibited and analyzed the items in the dossier, there still seems to be a necessity, recurrent and periodic, to set the defendants and accusers against each other once again in an unending trial in which there is, of course, no higher authority to which one might appeal.

What is difficult to unravel is whether this necessity is an emotional or a logical one. The tones are emotional, without a doubt, and the sources of these emotions ought to be interrogated. Both sides are far too emphatic for us not to inquire into the motives involved. But the basic theme is logical, since it involves nothing else, clearly, than legitimizing or delegitimizing a philosophy on the basis of the political commitment of its author. In any case, this is the underlying tendency of the debate—or of the confrontation, since the "affair" in question often appears as such.

This is only an underlying tendency, since most of the time both sides are ready to distinguish between levels and to introduce some reservations. But the global effect has nonetheless remained, for about twenty years now, the following: a major philosopher was a Nazi, and his philosophy is therefore virtually contaminated in every respect; or else it is necessary to claim that he was not a Nazi, or just barely, and only as a blunder, if we wish to maintain intact the image of a thought as pure as the Greek dawn whose brilliance it rediscovered.

It seems to me that the debate, in this state, itself harbors a philosophical and historical error, and that it is time to pull ourselves away from it, for the stakes are important.

But I am not going to dismiss the parties summarily without distinguishing between their arguments. Indeed, the defense shows quite clearly how a certain piety can blind one or push one into denial according to the Freudian formula, "Oh, I know, but still." The accusers, by contrast, take up the issues—except in a few rather crude cases—in a more frank and careful manner. Moreover, remarkable and penetrating analyses have been produced on this side, precisely because here the analysis has not been avoided on principle. Having said that, I do not want to go further into distinguishing and differentiating their works. Irrespective of persons, I would like to express my astonishment at this: Why is the question detached, or why does it appear to be detached, if not completely separated, from the condition of possibility, theoretical or historical, for such a grave political mistake on the part of such a philosopher?

(I note in passing that the same question should be posed with regard to Carl Schmitt, concerning whom we have recently seen sketched out the preludes of an analogous affair. These are certainly different cases, but they resemble one another.)

To pose the question in this way, we must first admit the political fault and at the same time the decisive importance of the thinker. From now on, I will argue on the basis of this double preliminary admission. The political fault cannot be disputed, nor can the importance of a philosophy whose mark is indelible, to say the least, on and through Sartre, Merleau-Ponty, Arendt, Bataille, Foucault, Derrida, Lacan, Granel, and many others.

How is it that this philosophy could set out, in 1933, down the path of the Third Reich? We can focus our analysis on one central problem, itself political or rather of direct political significance: a certain idea of the "people." We see clearly in *Being and Time* how the people come to take over from a "being-with" lost in anonymity and equivalence, in the undifferentiated mass that David Reisman would later call the "lonely crowd." The "people" could appear then as if they bore the possibility of recapturing a history, which is different from an entropic and melancholic scattering of "individuals," these countless mutilated multitudes of the modern world. More than anything else, Heidegger was sensitive to the modern turn—or fracture—of history (what constitutes the "modern" as such): the fact that history encountered its own obscuring without being able to return to the ahistorical modes represented by the diverse forms of continuity or eternity. (Rimbaud, the modern, already articulated for his time the desire for eternity.)

It will be objected, and rightly so, that the fascisms did not reopen any history but captured the technical and socioeconomic development of the modern in the immobile display of a dramatic and millenarian apotheosis. Heidegger quickly realized this, just as the Nazis realized that his discourse was hardly utilizable. However, Heidegger never stopped thinking stubbornly in a direction that would continue this initial vein. Why? One cannot get rid of this question without serious cost. And certainly not without all of us paying out of our own pockets.

I mean to say that no thought of this time—from Heidegger to us—has been able to recapture this question of history, but that everywhere around us today we can see it resurfacing and insisting, as the question of "democracy" or of the "world," as the question of the "event" or of what is left or not of "revolution," as the question of "sense" or of the "political"—all great signifiers of our aporias and our exigencies.

The question therefore is: What happened to history in the time of the fascisms? The answer is simple: it passed into the various forms of Marxism. The latter are thus characterized by a double disposition: of justice on the one hand, of history on the other. Between the two, there was a fissure, and perhaps this was already there with Marx. We can say, roughly, that justice was Kantian and history was Hegelian. Not only was there no conjunction, but history had become even more mechanical and anonymous than in Hegel himself. The "cunning of reason" was being given free rein. This is indeed what made up the intimate drama of so many thinkers for whom Marxism took a turn of thwarted desire (Benjamin and Bataille represent this most clearly). One could sum up thus: the crushing of the Spartakists in 1919–20 had its double or its symptom in an impasse encountered by the philosophies of history.

This is also what weighed upon the thought of those who began to form the Frankfurt School, since the foundation of the Institute by Horkheimer in 1923 (which is also the year when Lukács's *History and Class Consciousness* appeared). In those years, Marcuse, under the supervision of Heidegger, was writing his thesis, *Hegel's Ontology and the Theory of Historicity*. But Ernst Bloch's *The Spirit of Utopia* was already published in 1918, and it is possible to view the contrasts between these directions of thought as revealing the oppositions between an autonomous, mechanical or organic history, progressive without a subject, and the postulation of a subject who was not only the agent, but actually the effective term, here and now, of the march of history. History—history as actualization, as event, as what *comes* and *arises* [le *venir* et le *survenir*]— indeed no longer had any rightful heirs. Husserl, the least suspect of all the non-Marxists, still spoke in his lectures of 1935 of a "self-actualization" and a "self-illumination" of reason as the infinite movement of its progress. In 1935, Wittgenstein traveled in the Soviet Union and Freud was working on his *Moses and Monotheism*, which he called a "historical novel." *Civilization and Its Discontents* appeared in 1930. This gives an emblematic picture of the situation.

Of course, I do not wish to deny that there were those who opted for immediate struggle, those who were sent into exile (but they did not return from it with another history), and those who implacably denounced the infamy. The question to which I would like to limit my conclusion is precisely that of denunciation.

Denunciation is necessary. But so is enunciation. Heidegger enunciated a problem, and all his thought—on "being," "technics," or the "poem"—was a struggle with this problem. The stubborn or even obtuse obstinacy of this visceral reactionary is only the most visible face of a tenacity of thought that did not want to give up on this knot that I have called "history." The fact that he ended up evoking "a god," as we know—even this cannot be denounced without remainder. It was the terse and sharp statement of another aporia—but what matters above all is that this aporia or this knot is *ours*. This splinter falls into our garden. Whether it pleases us or not, we are concerned by it, for here before us, with or without Heidegger, history both continues to break apart and is happening once again.

28 February 2003

In the previous chronicle, I spoke of history: of the crisis or the aporia of history that the flat representations of progressivisms or the mythological frenzies of fascisms have echoed, but without providing a response. I wish to bring up today an indispensable corollary, which must be viewed under the concept or at least under the index of the *everyday*.

It was by contrast with the everyday that Heidegger brought up the exigency of history, and it was against the presumed "inauthenticity" or "improperness" of the former that he set up the no less presumptive "properness" or "authenticity" of a people capable of history. This pejorative attitude toward the everyday was anything but obvious, however, since this very everydayness was supposed to constitute the preontological ground of the ontological experience, that is, of "existing" in the strong sense. In other words, instead of standing firm on this ground, Heidegger ended up inverting daily coexistence into the solitude of being-toward-death, in order to overcome the latter in the historical community of a people. There was, then, no truth of the everyday that was not itself everyday and therefore banal, mediocre, and vulgar.

Later, however, in spite of Heidegger or because of him, we witness the resurgence of certain attempts to apprehend the everyday in a different way, as though out of a necessity that was felt as soon as one began to mistrust progressivisms as well as apotheoses or catastrophisms. There was something of this in Sartre, as there was in Henri Lefebvre and the situationists, or in other ways in Michel de Certeau or Foucault. Blanchot also pondered the difficulty of the everyday.

This difficulty is made manifest by the fact that it appears to be impossible not to submit the everyday sometimes to the infamy of insignificance and sometimes, in order to save it, to the hyper-significance of absorption into history, into the aesthetic, or even into the religious. In such an accession, the everyday loses its everydayness. The former can even be turned against the latter, by demanding a disruption of the course of life in order to convert it into ritual or into obsessional neurosis. It can also, most often, remain flatly quotidian. We can speak, with Hegel, of reading the newspaper as the "daily prayer of modern man." We can elevate the daily life of an epoch and a region to the dignity of a great historical subject. We can, like Perec, write *Life: A User's Manual*, or we can also, with or without psychoanalysis, convert the small change of our daily forgettings, delays, and slips into a signifying treasure. But nothing will prevent the wearing down of "the humble life of tedious, simple work," which erodes and disperses the exceptional moments without any hope of rescue.[5]

But must we *rescue* the everyday? Or, at least, must we rescue it by rescuing ourselves from it—by escaping it? And if this is not necessary, how can we think it without thinking in a mediocre manner (which is no longer to think)?

In other words, how can we think insignificance, if that is what constitutes the proper mark of the everyday?

As we know, Heraclitus invited his visitors to come into his kitchen, insisting that the gods could be found there, too. If these words have been reported, or invented, it's because they are part of a constant—one that is philosophical as well as political, religious, and aesthetic—according to which the true, the good, and the beautiful must as a general rule be linked to exception, to the brilliance of what appears only in sovereign conditions and whose corollaries are astonishment, an old philosophical virtue, or the respect that Kant calls a "feeling of reason." We want to feel that we are admiring the appearance of what exempts itself from a general dullness. In a certain way, all our versions of manifestation (the Platonic Idea, Husserlian transcendence, Christian revelation) are imprinted with this law of supreme distinction: the thing or truth should rise up and constitute an event, a coming-to-be. *Appearing* is a necessity for this register of thought, and all phenomenality, however modest, contains within it a reserve of the phenomenal in the sense of the spectacular.

The everyday, however, remains in its nonappearance. Or rather, it does not subsist in appearance as some hidden thing, but is itself nothing other than this nonappearance. It forms its nonapparent unfolding, or it weaves a nonappearing texture, and what appears is only a brief sparkle of this texture. What appears also disappears. But the nonapparent, for its part, persists—without, however, subsisting. As soon as we make it appear—in a thought, a painting (just as one used to speak of a "theater of everyday life")—we lose it, we make it come forth as an event, or we make an event spring up in contrast to it, eclipsing it.

But if the annulling of the everyday signals the event and its exception, the obstinacy of the everyday can also testify, not to an annulling of the event, but to the only real inscription that it is allowed. When *life goes on*—as Kiarostami's film aptly puts it[6]—and only when life goes on, can the event be inscribed. Only then, after the fact, does it take place. That is why, for example, there are two ways of accompanying the departure of the dead: with the suspension of and abstention from the everyday, or with its renewed affirmation. We fast, or else we eat; we are silent, or we talk. And sometimes both almost at the same time. In certain cultures, one returns to prepare a rustic meal on the tomb of the deceased, who is given his share of the food.

In an analogous manner, one mode of resistance that is most proper to the everyday is manifested during wars or other forms of catastrophe. I do not know if I can say this today, even as a blind history has unleashed a war in Iraq (on the eve of the day on which I am recording this chronicle). But I know that the emergence of the everyday in war, when this can happen, is what is most contrary to the goal of war—the internal goal, at least—insofar as war exemplifies the exception actualized and the excellence as much as the grandiloquence of heroism.

Perhaps, we must try to retain the language of what would not even be a modest heroism. For heroism always claims to stare down destiny, even if this means contemplating a terrible facelessness. But the everyday takes narrower and more secret and hidden paths, which are not for all that an evasive hiding away.

What the everyday hides is its own accession or its own hypostasis, as much as it hides the accession and hypostasis of a destiny or an absolute. In speaking of "the everyday" we do not succeed in naming any essence, or even an agency or authority, still less a truth, a good, or a beauty. Undoubtedly it happens, and it should happen, that the everyday is made into works [*fasse oeuvre*], and by means of these works it passes into exception and into its sovereign elevation. That is how Hegel saw in Flemish painting "the Sunday of life," and that is how, thanks to Andy Warhol, Campbell Soup has taken its place in the house of the Muses. In any case, the accession is limited, for it signals its own fugitiveness. The soup cans and the days pass by, whether they resemble each other or not, and their filing past drags the work into unworking [*désoeuvrement*].

Within the everyday, there subsists neither work, nor event, nor exception. Nothing of what constitutes law or faith. Or only the minimal forms of each of these, as though condensed or calcified. The law that says, "Every day has its share of grief," and the faith that says, "Tomorrow is another day." Empiricism and resignation, or a quiet resource for thinking otherwise? This is what must be put to the test.

One day it happens that grief reaches the point of giving up even the wait for tomorrow. That day is the most everyday of all. Its grief fills it without remainder, and "another day" becomes for it the other of all days, without, however, ceasing to be—as long as we have a glimpse of it—a day like any other. So even the exception, its law and its faith in the "sovereign instant," comes to be quite strangely confused with the everyday.

"Appearing" is confounded with "disappearing," or, in a more subtle way, it shows itself as never having appeared in truth. Nonappearance is immobilized. At the same time, at the same instant, a life appears for an instant in its singular exception, and it rejoins the nonappearance of all other lives, those of the dead as well as those of the living. We might say that nonapparent lives as a whole are eternalized without any brilliant manifestation, but also without annulling their works or their truths. Spinoza says that we experience our character as eternal beings. We must add that this is an everyday experience, which immediately means that this experience does not appear to us.

28 March 2003

The previous chronicle was simultaneous with the beginning of what one calls "war": today's chronicle is contemporaneous with the immediate postwar situation. Within a month an act has been performed that has serious chances of eventually becoming a landmark, both symbolic and real, in retracing the history of the great turn that the world has been experiencing for about thirty years. Revolving or toppling over, transformation or collapse, we are unable to decide, for it is no longer possible for us to believe that we can master a clearly marked course of history.

That's also why it is impossible for us to seek to presume that behind the invasion of Iraq there is some sort of Hegelian "cunning of reason," as some people have ventured to assert. For in order to be able to maintain such a presumption, there must be two presuppositions: on the one hand, that American democracy represents reason in the process of its self-development; and on the other hand, that this presumed rationality can, in the end, be transplanted outside of America.

To the extent that it is forbidden for us to be Hegelian in this sense, we are also not allowed to be beautiful souls. But there are certain motivations to fear this danger: the indignation aroused by the war—amplified to an exceptional degree by the force of a world public opinion that is rarely so consensual—is likely to act as a lure and a trap. Now I certainly do not mean that we should not be indignant. This invasion is loathsome, cynical, and brutal. Thousands of deaths, and many more injured and orphaned, the thirst and the pain of the Iraqi people, the humiliated grief of the "Arab nation" (as one used to say), the devastation of the testimony provided by our early writings and our earliest cosmogonies, not to mention the tearing open of Europe, all these cry for justice—and the cry is all the greater since this desolation is carried out with a crude assurance that is quite properly barbaric and that would be pitiful if one could feel any pity for this outburst.

But what may risk functioning as a lure is the system of accusation that points to absolute American evil as the sudden emergence of Satan in a Texan hat. This accusation sometimes reaches the point, among Arabs, of referring to "Nazism" and "totalitarianism"; everywhere it is directed at the figure of George W. Bush, who is attacked as a preacher full of fury. Either way, one is far from inquiring into the real issue behind the event.

The lure begins with the word "war." We should have known for a long time now (Carl Schmitt diagnosed it from the so-called first "world" war) that there is no war in the real sense whenever a claim is made to an international policing mechanism, whether it be economic, strategic, moral, or all of these together. There is then the assumption of a globally applicable right, but one whose jurisprudence as well as its effective operation are in the command of a single power (abetted by those who submit to it). It is no longer the right that governed relations between sovereign states; rather, it is the law that a virtually global democracy arrogates to itself as the law of what is not even an "empire," in truth, but rather a general enterprise of logistics. This logistics is regulated according to an interminable a priori calculation of the increase of means without ends implemented by a two-sided self-productive power: the self-production of technics and the self-production of cost as general equivalence. It is a matter of management and, in fact, every bomb will have been an investment.

This used to be called capital, and we no longer have the right to be lured into believing that it can be reduced to the name of Bush or Wolfowitz. Capital, on the contrary, informs us better than ever of its anonymity. For the rest, we know how the names of Saddam Hussein himself, of Bin Laden, and so many other political and religious names of the Arab world, not to mention other names from other worlds, become fused together within this anonymity.

We should also not be lured into ignoring the fact that capital is self-produced and is self-reproduced also as "democracy," while at the same time being baptized as divine service. In Iraq, after all, democracy today is crushing the remnants of what in the beginning was the Baath party's attempt to introduce, in the time and in the shadow of so-called "real" socialism, a democratic modernity. In a parallel manner, the invocations of God under one name or another do nothing but reveal more clearly what is in fact the religious essence of a politics that wants to submit and, strictly speaking, to sacrifice our diversity to the foundational Unity of an indefinitely self-productive equivalence, or of an indefinitely tautological equivalence, as one may wish to call it.

In other words, we no longer have the right to delude ourselves regarding the fact that for the past thirty-odd years the process of capital has been conspicuously eliminating and eroding everything that, in principle, was promising in our democracies and our (a)theologies, even if some of these promises required a rigorous internal deconstruction. The movement since the Second World War can be summarized as follows: unable to strengthen democracy and atheism, we have given or abandoned our rights to the powerful forces of a single theodemocracy, which is tearing itself apart under the cover of a supposed "war of civilizations."

This self-management of barbarism, in which we are all caught up (French and German politics are not exempt from it, after all), forbids us to be deluded about something essential: the words *democracy* and *atheism* no longer refer to anything solid, no more than do *socialism* or *religious faith*. Let us not imagine that we can denounce the war on the basis of a peace guaranteed by significations. As for words and concepts, we must remake them all. Sense is before us like a night into which we must enter with eyes wide open and which neither Enlightenment, nor Revelation, nor the flash of blasting weapons can illuminate.

25 April 2003

This chronicle could be given the title "On the Possible Use of Negativity." Before beginning it, I pause to say that I am speaking on the day after an earthquake in Algeria, which has left at least a thousand people dead according to first estimates, and more than seven thousand wounded. My reasons for mentioning this will soon be clear.

Two weeks ago, in the building next to where I live, a man died in his house, alone, and was discovered only after several days. Some time earlier, elsewhere in the city, a young man had died under the same conditions. A neighbor in my block wanted to know how many people die in this way, isolated from all presence, deprived of any testimony to the last moment, this moment whose witnesses, when there are any, are the first in charge of the mourning, the first ministers of this service thanks to which we bring into our midst the void that can no longer be admitted among us or received anywhere at all.

Death without possible mourning has always befallen those who disappeared without witnesses, or died by extermination, whose witnesses have so often been stricken in their capacity, or in the very sense of their position, as witnesses.

Hidden death, which is, in a way, the death of death, the negation of the inclusion or inscription of death in life (in language), has perhaps become a social or cultural fact (let us add here medicalized hospital death, where the only witness is the recording apparatus). If human culture began with the testimonial inscription of death, then in our day this culture is perhaps vacillating on its most extreme point.

This can be stated in another way, and with a further elaboration: we are ill at ease with negativity.

We are obsessed with death, war, science, absence, emptiness, solitude, excess, and infinity, and it is a bad obsession, for in it a morbid vertigo seems to be combined with the impossibility of inscribing them in an economy, that is to say, also in an ecology, and, in general, in an *oikos*, in a dwelling, in a habitation, and within a familiarity (which is something other than familiality).

The evidence for this impasse is precisely the fact that the word "economy" means to us nothing more than the "icy waters of selfish calculation" [Marx, *Capital*], whereas the word *ecology* floats on the same waters devoid of compass and concept.

That is why, on every side, we rail against nihilism, against negativism, against all forms of retreat, suspension, finitude, or impossibility, judged wrongly or rightly—and most often wrongly and confusedly—to be either morbid or suicidal. In their place, we ask for affirmation or value, decision and resolve, and from this perspective a symmetrical haziness could suggest that one wishes at all cost to *be positive*, to use an expression that has been forged, by no means at random, by advertising.

Between positivation and negation—equally uni-lateral and abstract—between these, or rather over and above their opposition, itself no less simple and abstract, is another attitude possible?

As we know, Hegelian dialectic has represented the moment that can be spoken of as the full employment of negativity. I say "full employment" thinking of Bataille's expression "unemployed negativity" [*negativité sans emploi*], an expression in which we might still find a formula useful to us.

Hegelian dialectic supposes a transformation of negativity into a positivity raised above the level of positive immediacy. Death is engendered in it as the life of the Spirit, and devastation prepares the way for a further blossoming. But today we know of a negativity without any transformation or blossoming.

That is why we can say that after Hegel there is no other major philosophical problem than that of transforming the dialectic, of displacing it, replacing it, rupturing it, or deconstructing it. Whether it is a matter of revolution, or of hidden death, of love or art, or of economics, the structure of the problem is the same: there is an excess of negativity, a loss or a remainder in surplus, something supernumerary in relation to all calculation that it is impossible for us to submit to reason. In a sense, technics has the character and the structure of this indefinite waste or loss: it disassembles, destroys, and displaces, not in order to remake, but in order to displace further; thus it is not governed by the possible but by the repeated possibilization of the unprecedented (performing more, informing more, transforming more).

But perhaps this is not as new as we might believe. If the death that is hidden from testimony is bitter and cynical in the midst of our never-extinguished networks of communication, at the same time this cannot fail to remind us that death was always hidden—and along with it love, meaning, knowledge, and the divine.

If it is necessary to place ourselves within affirmation—and it is necessary, without any doubt, according to an imperative which is that of thought itself (I would dare say that thought, like the Freudian unconscious, is in fact unaware of negation, since it is always at least the power to affirm the negative)—if it is thus necessary, then, to affirm, then may our affirmation be precisely an affirmation of the impossible.

In affirming the impossible, we do not dialecticize it, we do not domesticate it, we do not transform it into the possible, and yet we also do not fall into the trap of nihilist despair.

If I affirm as impossible the recuperation, the re-appropriation of death, of love, of justice, or of beauty, I do not fall into the melancholy of a lost or absent possibility: on the contrary, I affirm that the impossible itself is the price of death, of love, of justice, and of truth. Here, instead of the impossible (the negative) being swallowed by affirmation and made positive in it, it is affirmation that is inscribed in the impossible.

And this too is not new for philosophy. When Plato leads Theaetetus up to the point of knowing that knowledge of knowledge is not given, he reveals two faces of the same aporia. On the one hand, the knowledge of impossibility, with the necessity of an absence, a mourning, a renunciation. But on the other hand, the impossible as knowledge: a knowledge of self as knowledge without object, and therefore all the more subject, but subject *of* nothing and subject *to* nothing, "such that into itself eternity finally changes it" [Mallarmé, "The Tomb of Edgar Poe"]. The exact subject of a coincidence with the self so extreme that it becomes the vacuity of a point.

Philosophy has always known and always practiced (even with Hegel, if we were to read him a little better) this exactness, which does not transform negativity, but which punctuates it, which pricks it or pins it on pages covered with our feverish writings, our discourses and our poems. That's what is beautiful—with a true beauty that is not satisfying but extenuating.

Can I hope that by telling you this, by giving these words over to chance and to the hazard of your listening, I am rendering some justice, however minute, to this unknown neighbor whose death was hidden from us? A justice rendered to him and therefore to *us*, that is to say, to the possibility never assured, always risked, of uttering this "we" which entrusts all of us to the impossible.

23 May 2003

The season of festivals, biennials, and other art fairs and markets has revived here and there the furious quarrel ignited about twenty years ago around what we call, in a singular manner, contemporary art. The most manifest sense of this expression, "contemporary art," is to designate an art constantly in tune with its own debate, contemporary with its own questioning or its own suspension; in short, contemporary with this distancing from itself, with this intimate dissociation that one must have in order to experience oneself, in whatever domain, as the "contemporary" of something or someone.

I like this quarrel, whose violence simultaneously reveals and conceals the importance of the issue—it reveals this importance through its intensity, but often conceals it with the noise it makes. Let us try to discern, without making too much noise, the importance of what's at stake. "Art" is the name for a practice with a double specificity: on the one hand, it can be identified, in the final instance, only in terms of works (productions, constructions, creations, tangible things) and not in terms of categorized objects (as would be the case with knowledge, power, salvation, happiness, justice, etc.); on the other hand, this practice has its unity only in the diversity of its concrete modalities (painting, music, cinema, performance, etc.). The specificity of "art" is thus found twice over in exteriority and in diversity, or even in disparity: it has neither the categorial unity of the object, nor the intuitive unity of the sensible work. Nonetheless, there's a certain unity, a certain "unitary" content designated precisely by the word "art"—a word that, taken in this sense, has been around for barely two centuries, as we know (but the history of this word undoubtedly marks out a great shift in history as such, even if the "one" thing found in "art" is as old as humanity: the early life of this word evokes a power that has been nurtured from the very beginning . . .).

The manifest and obscure sense of the word *art* is precisely what foments the quarrel. It is the sense of an impossible unity, the sense of a missing sense. Or rather, it is a lack of sense that never ceases making sense, obstinately—at the very least the sense of this quarrel that furiously argues over its proper character in exclamations divided up among various voices: "This is art!" or "This is not art!" or "What actually is art?"

We learn something essential from this: among the various human activities, there is one practice whose meaning cannot be categorized (submitted to a signification) but whose sensible effectivity is always both irreducibly multiple and compellingly necessary: this necessity, indeed, is not that of individuals who wish to be "artists" without being conjointly that of a common world that wants to enjoy works of art (whether it be popular art or, on the contrary, esoteric art is another question).

We could say this: we have an exigency to give ourselves the sense or the feeling—together and each by himself—of an overflow of meaning. We have the desire to sense and to feel according to a truth that no meaning can saturate (neither knowledge, nor salvation, nor justice, etc.) and that no unity can sublimate.

Thus contemporary art, with its quarrel, brings forth a desire that is neither the desire for an object nor the desire for a meaning but a desire for feeling and for feeling oneself feel—a desire to experience oneself as irreducible to a signification, to a being or an identity. A desire to enjoy, in sensibility, the very fact that there is no unique and final form in which this desire would reach its end.

Perhaps psychoanalysis provides us a valuable clue about this desire. Not by attempting to analyze art—we know all too well the poor results of such attempts—but on the contrary, by describing art, or at least the artistic gift, as "unanalyzable," as Freud insisted on several occasions. The unanalyzable character of this gift corresponds to the fact that the work of art appears in the place of the symptom, as he also says. Replacing the symptom means moving out of the order of interpretation. A work of art is the failure or the disconnection of interpretation (or its infinite rebeginning and opening up, which amounts to the same). The work of art is thus akin to the "navel of the dream," which Freud refers to as the point at which interpretation will and must be lost without return. (I add here, mischievously, that Freud himself refers to analysis as an "art of interpretation" . . . which should then appear as the formula of a contradiction—unless, pushing a bit further, we can deduce from it that art is, in the final account, the desire and/or the dream of Freud and of psychoanalysis as a whole . . . which thus becomes a symptom for the contemporary period . . .)

The desire for art—like the dream-wish, and perhaps, if I dare say, like the dream-wish of the community or, if you prefer, of the "us"—would then be the desire beyond every sensible object, the desire for the sense of desire itself. Spinoza perhaps would have recognized in it his *conatus*, Nietzsche his will to eternal return, Heidegger his decision of existence . . .

But, at the same time, no philosopher could adhere to this without also eventually freeing himself from the greed for *knowledge* contained in his concept of desire. A philosopher or an analyst, as much as an epistemologist, a theologian, or a political scientist, encounters at this limit the insistence of a nonknowledge, the impulse and the pulsation of a nescience, multiple and sensible by nature, which is the only way to comprehend the *denouement of sense* that must be apprehended in every possible sense. What is taken in charge in this denouement, in this unbinding that creates a sensible work, is nothing less than the energy that brings us into the world, that puts us in relation to ourselves, each one and everyone together, in a silent protest against all imposition of sense and in the affirmation of a speech always moving beyond itself and directed against every form of "last word" that would like to fix the truth.

Freud used to say that he could say nothing of music, not even analyze it, as he believed he could do with painting. He thus reluctantly recognized that what approaches speech without taking on signification, what allows us to *hear* [entendre] how it is a matter of *listening* without understanding [*entendre*] anything, what proposes a presence in a state of permanent imminence and thus in the rhythmic repetition of its effacement, of its slipping away— that this and this alone is what opens our ears, as well as our eyes, and every part of us that can be open.

27 June 2003

July twenty-fifth: this is the last chronicle. One could call it supernumerary. Besides, I did not know, a month ago, that it was planned. Even though I hardly stop working in summer, I did not imagine that philosophy would continue on the radio until almost the beginning of August. With an altogether academic ingenuousness, I was reasoning as though the sun should place thought in suspension . . .

But we know that the exact opposite is the case. Thought has suspended the sun ever since it launched the earth in motion around it. More exactly, having ceased to "rescue the phenomena" and to explain the appearances, calculating thought has related the celestial bodies and their movements to the general ordering of an expanding universe where suns proliferate, frozen as well as incandescent ones, apparent and nonapparent ones . . .

This has hardly shaken the congenital heliocentrism of our thought, however. *Occidental*, as we say and as it called itself, which means "declining" or "falling" (in Greek, Latin or Arabic), this thought is still represented in a fatal distancing in relation to an "Orient," which is to say, to a birth or a sunrise. Or else it has seen itself as turning or turned back toward this Orient, reoriented toward a sun that it took for itself, whose *Lumières* or Enlightenment it caused to rise by means of its own forces.

We are so accustomed to the recurrent catachresis of light and sun that we no longer pay much attention to it. It is taken for granted that knowledge, truth, right, and beauty are luminous.

However, photocentrism and heliocentrism do not amount to the same, and this too we know— but this knowledge is more obscure, which is not by chance. The metaphors of light, clarity, and evidence, like those of transparency or limpidity, are related to the order of vision. The visible comes to be discerned by a correct dividing up [*partage*] of light and darkness. Even if it is still a matter of progressively dissipating all obscurities, one accepts the necessity of a dark region, concerning which one says that there is no question of reaching it.

It is yet another matter with the sun itself. If one thinks about it for a moment, one realizes that the sun exceeds the logic and the gnoseology of the visible. From Plato up to Nietzsche at least, our culture was also ordered according to the desire or the will to go beyond the luminous visible in order to consider the luminous source (in Latin *lux*, distinct from *lumen*). The latter cannot be divided by any shadow, and that is why the early observations of dark spots on the sun were charged with blasphemous impiety—an accusation in which, bizarrely, Apollo came to shelter the God of Abraham, who preferred to be enveloped in clouds.

For Plato, the sun is the *analogon* of the Good in the visible world, and what it communicates to mundane realities is not only luminous visibility but also generative and nourishing warmth. The brilliance of this metaphysical sun shines all the way up to Hegel and Nietzsche, but we should also discern it in everything that corresponds to the concept of an "intellectual intuition" or an "originary gifting vision": that is to say, whenever the subject is not merely the one who recognizes objects in the light, but the one who makes them appear in his light and because of it.

In philosophy, this sun no doubt gives form to the metamorphosis of the divine—which is almost always primordially solar in the mythologies out of which philosophy emerged. And, of course, a residual scoria of this star and of its sacred or even sacrificial power was also formed. Insofar as the sun is not sight, as Plato emphasizes, it cannot itself be seen without bedazzlement—and it is Plato who attests to this as well. When, on the contrary, sight is represented as originary and giving, it must be called "vision" in quotation marks, "penetrating vision" or "insight" (*Ein-sicht* in German), or else "evidence," this great word of a tradition that, from Descartes to Husserl, made an effort to fix the point where sight surges forth as its own light.

Now, this point is necessarily blind, and the tradition knows this too. In the order of the solar *analogon*, one cannot look at the daytime star without burning one's eyes. A tearing contraction is produced at the point of evidence: the eye is destroyed by the sun that thus comes out of it. It is this coincidence that is willed—Nietzsche's "noon," the moment of the greatest thought, "exactly under the sun," as Gainsbourg sings so well—it is the *solstice* that is awaited, and when it happens, the sun darkens in its own vision. It is just the same with our metaphysics in general as with the sundance of the Dakota Indians: the dancers look at the sun while pulling at the strings hooked to their skin until the latter rips open. (But today, on summer beaches, do not people offer their skin to dangerous blades of bronze?)

It is well known that La Rochefoucauld repeated this maxim of the ancients: "Neither the sun nor death can be looked directly in the face." But perhaps the question is: What thing *can* be looked at directly in the face? If looking something "in the face" means seeing its "truth" or "evidence," then there is never any direct face-to-face. Every face is a bedazzlement, terrible and marvelous.

Soleil cou coupé ("Neck-severed sun"): this famous line from Apollinaire summarizes it all.[7] The sun is a bloody slice that interrupts discourse and every order constructed as a body. A slice and a sharp edge, in the absolute coincidence of its evident burning in which the gaze, in effect, is hollowed out, *sees itself hollowed out* [se voit évidé]. That is the end but also the beginning of the poem. Homer, thus, was blind.

25 July 2003

Notes

NOTE: All notes have been supplied by the translator.

1. The French word *chronique* means both "chronicle" (noun) and "chronic" (adjective) in English. Thus, *chronique philosophique* means "philosophical chronicle" and *maladie chronique* means "chronic illness."

2. The connections among this series of words, all of which begin with *auto* ("self"), including *automobile*, are more apparent in French than in English.

3. "In the Homeric works, *Moira* is the personification of Destiny, the power that determines the fate of man from the time of his birth. It imposes itself even on the gods and above all, Zeus; sometimes it appears identical to their will and one thinks that they can transgress it." *La Grande Encyclopédie*, vol. 23, s.v. "Moira."

4. In French, the word *politique* is used both as an adjective ("political") and as a substantive ("politics"). The meaning of the word as substantive also changes according to

whether it is feminine (*la politique*) or masculine (*le politique*). *La politique* can mean either "politics" as an activity or "policy," while *le politique* refers to the domain of politics, as opposed, for example, to that of social welfare (*Harrap's Unabridged French-English Dictionary*).

5. Paul Verlaine, *Sagesse* (*Wisdom*), bk. 1, poem 8; this is the first line.

6. The reference is to Abbas Kiarostami's film titled *La vie continue* in French and *Life and Nothing More* in English.

7. The quote is the last line of the poem entitled "Zone."